Funeral for a Stranger

BECCA STEVENS
Funeral for a Stranger
thoughts on life and love

Abingdon Press / Nashville

Funeral for a Stranger: Thoughts on Life and Love

This book is printed on acid-free paper.

Library of Congress Cataloging-in-Publication Data

Stevens, Becca, 1963-
    Funeral for a stranger / Becca Stevens.
        p. cm.
    ISBN 978-1-4267-0244-0 (pbk. : alk. paper)
    1. Death—Religious aspects—Christianity. 2. Funeral rites and ceremonies.
I. Title.
    BT825.S795 2009
    264'.030985—dc22

                                    2009011235

Scripture quotations are from the Book of Common Prayer, 1979.

09 10 11 12 13 14 15 16 17 18—10 9 8 7 6 5 4 3

MANUFACTURED IN THE UNITED STATES OF AMERICA

contents

I am like all the other
back sides of maple leaves
sitting in this forest
except that you see me as different.
You celebrate the changing
seasons in me.
I know when fall comes
and I return to earth,
you will water that patch of ground
with your tears.
Except for love,
I would fall without
a sound.

Becca Stevens

ONE

the call

I was the minister for her funeral because I hate to say no. As an Episcopal priest, I'm not obligated to bury people who are not part of my congregation. I had received a message from the family asking me to bury their mother. I had planned to call them back and make a polite excuse, saying I was sorry I couldn't help. Then I was going to give them the number of a United Methodist minister who helps me when I get busy. Before I had time to call them back, though, the minister called me and said he wasn't available. I hate the idea of someone getting left out, especially in crisis, so when the family called again, I just said, "I would love to help."

Less than twenty-four hours later, I was driving to the visitation to meet the daughter and regretting my openness to the whole thing. I knew how much energy I had to invest to be present pastorally, and I was feeling the weight of a congregation that needed tending and charitable organizations to manage. I also thought about how the trip across town was going to ruin any hope of seeing my family that night. A wave of guilt washed over me. I wanted to be a good priest and a good mom. Most of the time the two roles complement and inform each other, but sometimes they are in direct conflict.

"Okay," I thought resolutely, "I will get there, take some notes on this person whose name I have now totally forgotten, and try to get back home in time for the end of dinner." I am not sure how conversations happen inside my head. They seem to bubble up with possible solutions presenting themselves in the midst of all the information. Then, once I figure out a way to move forward, the conversations rest in peace for awhile.

I get that ability from my mom. She raised five children as a single parent while directing a community center. She must have had thousands of conversations in her head while driving between meetings at the office and running children around town. My mom would walk through the front door after work and tell us what was going to happen that evening or the next day. There were never any real discussions or attempts to work out problems as a group. By the time the words came out of her mouth, it was a done deal. Our job was to get in line and carry out the plan so that everything could get done in the shortest amount of time.

This is a great example of how I didn't want to be like my mom. Even as I was driving, though, I could see myself running into the house, just as my family was beginning to relax, and delivering the list of orders: begin homework, let the dogs out, turn off the TV "for the love of God," and head toward the dirty dishes in the sink. I hope someday my children, when they have children of their own and are behind at work and late getting home, will realize that my head conversations helped me feel as if I still had control over my life. I hope they will know that in those conversations, they were the central characters, and they were loved the whole time I was figuring out how we could make our family work.

The person who gets the worst of it is my husband, Marcus. After my head conversations, I forget I never actually told him what was planned. His life is already full, so it's hard for him when I change things to make it all work for me. Thank God he is used to this after twenty years. He knows that if he waits it out, another conversation will follow in my head and plans will change again to accommodate him.

Sometimes I count these head conversations as prayers. I don't think they should count, but I count them anyway because I don't pray enough. Sometimes God is a part of my silent discussions, even though I don't give God an actual voice. God feels present when there is some clarity of thought or when I feel a little peace after struggling with an issue.

To be honest, I am not sure how people have conversations with God, where God has an actual voice. I'm not saying it isn't possible, but it's always awkward for me to listen as people report these conversations. I once heard a woman from Honduras talk about a conversation with God in which she spoke and then God said, "Va," which means "Go." It struck me that God, as reported by the woman, spoke Spanish with a perfect accent, which made it sound like "Ba," kind of a sheep sound. I knew that God would never say "Ba" to me because I would giggle and not listen. There have been beautiful and faithful people who have said God tells them what to get at the grocery store, whom to date, and what to wear. That God has a voice different from theirs is hard for me to grasp. The God of their understanding is much more detailed than the God of my understanding. Sometimes the stories leave me feeling as though God is less than God and not the author of life and love. I am a little cynical and skeptical about it all.

So I'm usually content to leave God as the force of love pulling all the millions of silent conversations all over the world toward love. God needs to keep pulling my conversations toward love, especially in motherhood. I love my kids so much, and I hate that sometimes I bark orders tersely instead of saying, "I am sorry that I missed dinner and now it's too late to make up that time: What's on TV?"

The private conversation in the car that day took place before I even arrived at the funeral home to meet the family. Just the idea of a funeral can get my mind going full throttle. Funerals startle our minds from the lull of living. When all of a sudden we are made to think about death, close range, we come to ourselves. A funeral takes precedence in our day as other, routine events get changed to make room. This mirrors what happens internally when we are going to a funeral. All the other thoughts move to the side to make room for thoughts like, *Oh my God, we are all mortal, life is a gift, and someday there will be a funeral for me.*

The journey toward a funeral begins with thoughts about those we love who have died, those we love who are still with us, and I think, "what we think we would want if we died now." It's natural and makes life come into focus a little more clearly as our minds and bodies and spirits jolt into consciousness. The goal is to try to sift through most of these thoughts before we arrive at the funeral so we may be present for those grieving who were closest to the person who died.

What I didn't realize before the drive was that all this quickening of thought happens whether or not we know the person. Already thoughts are flooding my mind about my mother, who has been dead for over a decade; about Uncle John, who died twenty years ago; about my husband and children, who I pray will outlive me; and about how to avoid a funeral home when I die. Just the act of anticipating the funeral and getting ready to meet a grieving daughter has undone me a bit. I can feel my heart and mind opening and the most basic and important questions of faith rising in me. Presiding at this funeral has already reminded me to think about my priorities and my family. Already this funeral is a gift, and I haven't even walked through the door.

T W O

cups of coffee

I arrived before the visitation began so I could plan the service with the daughter of the stranger who had died. When I walked in, the grieving daughter was sitting close to a friend who ended up doing most of the talking. The two women said they were best friends and that they had lived together for more than a decade. They were the caregivers for the mother who had died, and when she was too sick to care for herself, both the daughter and the best friend had moved to the mother's home to care for her.

Within fifteen minutes of my meeting these two wonderful and compassionate women, new thoughts were born in my head. Now my thoughts were about how I could help them get through this with as much grace and dignity as possible. I wanted to help them make a really fine funeral for the mother.

It was during that initial meeting that I started trying to piece together the family history. It occurred to me that maybe they were strangers to every minister in the region because some time ago their family had been estranged from the church. Maybe someone had been a freethinker and just couldn't accept the Christianity that was preached at them. Maybe years and years ago a pastor had abused someone. Maybe someone had grown sick of hearing pastors who had forgotten that the biggest moral issue facing the church is the suffering of others. Maybe God, in a private conversation, had told someone, "Va."

They told me the mother had been a Methodist but hadn't been inside a church in decades. While the daughter and her friend related the story of the mother's faithful life as a worker, wife, and mother, I was compelled to create an under-story for myself. I still didn't know much about the story of their lives. It may have had something to do with these two beautiful women sitting beside me. Churches are masters at estranging people. They have excommunicated, ostracized, shunned, labeled, and damned people to hell since they started organizing in Antioch. Some time ago, the mother must have slowly broken the last thin ties she may once have had with the church. I wonder if the members of her church ever talked to her about why she left. I wonder if she left that last Sunday service over twenty years ago without words. I wonder if she had grown to be a stranger in that community, or if she had always felt like one. I wonder if anyone had called her and said they missed her. I wonder if she felt close to God and knew God loved her. I hope so.

Our communities are broken. That is why the prayer of community always includes a request to mend the brokenness among us as well as within ourselves. The problem occurs when relationships are severed permanently. That is when strangers are born. After years and generations, we no longer recognize one another or mourn our broken past.

Once I went through the door and met the only daughter who was burying her only surviving parent, I was reminded of the great harm that comes with cutting ourselves off from one another. It's hard to reconnect. It's impossible to make up for all the lost time. We didn't start out as strangers in our faith; we began as family. But now we are estranged from most of the people we encounter in our daily routines or on the news. From a distance, there seems to be no obligation or sense of community. We have no real desire or need to help the man on the street or the woman overseas who is displaced. We are responsible only for the people within our self-defined circles. That is how we draw lines and protect our boundaries. If we would just look closer, though, I think we would realize that those lines of separation are razor-thin. We are really all connected: spiritually, physiologically, and socially.

Last summer I traveled to a small town in New Mexico and wandered into a bookstore and café. Two women in their forties were sitting with a cup of coffee and sharing a piece of cake. As I walked by, one woman said, "I told her she needs to stay in therapy." The other woman nodded in sympathy. I could easily have bought a cup of coffee, pulled up another seat, and joined in the conversation about their mutual friend who was going through hard times. "The ruts are deep after twenty years," I might have chimed in, or "I wish her children would cut her some slack."

As I paid for a book and left the store, I thought about how those women were no more strangers than my own friends. Such conversations happen in every town in America where women gather to walk through the stages of life together and reach out for support and comfort. Women share cups of coffee or tea, talk about their worries for their friends or family, and seek allies to share the burden of loving care.

These conversations also take place in other languages with different nuances all over the world. During the past couple of years, I have joined in on a few in Egypt, Ecuador, and Rwanda. The conversations link me to women everywhere, each woman casting a wide net across her relationships with family, friends, and work. I can imagine that, through this intricate and binding web, most of the world is connected by a million women sipping coffee in groups of two and three. Where two or three are gathered, God's spirit is present.

Last year a small group of women from Tennessee met with a small group of women from Rwanda who were trying to leave the streets and return to their community. The journey from living on the streets back into interdependence with others is like a trip across a vast desert and into a promised land. It is mysterious and hard. One of the women leading our group was a graduate of Magdalene in Nashville, a two-year recovery program for women who have survived lives of violence, addiction, and prostitution. I founded the program in 1997 with two hopes: I wanted a program based on the truth that love is the most powerful force in the world for social change, and I wanted to create a sanctuary for the women where they could live for two years without having to pay for it. Now Magdalene has a full staff, a business called Thistle Farms, and several homes.

A group from Rwanda had contacted us to see if we could help them start a program similar to the one in Nashville. Sure, we said, we would love to come and see how we could make some new friends. We brought about twenty letters from women in Nashville to read to the women of Kigali. In those letters, the Nashville women told their stories, describing the connections between the buying and selling of women and the drug market, telling how sexual abuse is a generation older than prostitution. As we read the letters, the women from Rwanda all nodded. Their stories were hauntingly similar. The particular suffering of women on the streets doesn't belong to one community or nation. It moves freely over oceans and into every culture. The women from the streets of Nashville and Kigali share a history, a story, and a hope.

We were reminded on that trip that rape and love are universal languages that people experience individually. Neither gets lost in translation. Our job is to remember we are family, not strangers, and to love universally, one individual at a time. It is an amazing task to take on, loving the whole world an individual at a time.

We visited many sites in Rwanda where whole communities had been wiped out in the genocide. A million people died, one at a time, in the spring of 1994. When guides told the stories, I could feel a throbbing in the front of my head, as if it couldn't take in the pain being described. When we tried to sleep, our legs would shake from the overwhelming information we had received. Still, I kept thinking, all we can do is keep trying to love people, even if it feels as if we are using a thimble to drain water out of the ocean.

I stood at one holocaust site where the guide described ongoing efforts to find bodies that the killers had buried in unmarked graves so that people wouldn't find them. When I started crying, I felt unworthy to have tears. Who in the hell did I think I was to cry, since I couldn't even imagine the scale of the suffering? The only answer I could come up

with was this: Who in the hell must people think they are
not to cry?

We are all connected. When we deny it and create a
world full of strangers, we are silently condoning violence.
We can no longer imagine or feel sympathy for what the
stranger must be going through. In a culture of strangers,
anger and misunderstanding and ignorance of one another
thrive. Once we get to "them" and "us," it is hard to stand
on common ground.

For example, in 2000, in the state of Tennessee, we
started executing prisoners again after a forty-year hiatus.
There is a handful of people who protest the act by going to
a field near the prison on the night of an execution. It is an
eerie feeling to stand in the dark with a candle and pray for
someone you have never met who is a criminal and who is
about to die. I am compelled to go as a way to honor life
itself and to hold up principles over individual personalities.
The protest seems inconsequential in some ways, but I have
to do it. I have to believe that killing is wrong, period. I
have to protest, because if I won't stand and hold a candle
for a stranger in the name of life, maybe it all doesn't mean
that much anyway.

The majority of people in the state are completely oblivious to what is going on. Maybe for most of them it is not a matter of craving blood for blood but more a feeling that the death of a criminal they don't know is not important. It is always disturbing on the morning after an execution to walk my child to school. Maybe it's a bright, sunny day, and other moms, who are strangers, smile as they pass. I am tired from standing and holding a candle, and I wonder, *Do you care that the state murdered someone while we were sleeping?*

THREE

goldie the fish

After my talk with the daughter and her friend, I stopped thinking of the funeral as a burden. I wanted to bring out my best effort for these strangers in the hope of reconciling myself as a minister of the church to this family. I wanted the family to know there are Christians who are nonjudgmental, who don't worry about making an equation out of belief and salvation. I really liked the daughter and wanted to be present to this family I didn't know but was beginning to love. I can't explain it any better than that.

Once I was in this new mind-set of celebrating a funeral for a stranger, the idea that she was a stranger began to feel like a luxury. Somehow the idea of not knowing her and beginning to care about her was a gift. It felt as though the act of jumping into this with my heart, without any knowledge of the mom before she died, might offer me a glimpse into the universal truth of grief itself.

After I finished making plans with the daughter, the service started to feel like a calling from God, what we are asked to do as part of humanity: to love the stranger, tend the sick, comfort the sorrowful, and bury the dead. Love was growing in me, along with a sense of hope for myself and this small part of the world. In living out our faith, we don't have to know one another literally; we just have to love one another spiritually. We are called to comfort one another. We can empathize and remember what it was like to grieve ourselves. Grief is one of our most universal feelings. Everyone knows and respects its power and depth.

I have been amazed by the power of grief. In my life it has been one of the defining ways that I make sense of the world. It is my first memory, and I have grieved big and small things for as long as I can remember. When I was five years old, my father was killed by a drunk driver on my mom's birthday. It was November 22, 1968, at 11:15 a.m. The ordeal etched itself into my memory with such vividness and detail, it pretty much left no room for other memories. I remember what people were wearing at the funeral, and afterward what it was like to have to go to the bathroom with the house packed full of people. I remember worrying if we would still get presents for Christmas. My four siblings say the same thing: the grief was so sudden and powerful, it became a defining moment in all our lives.

So it was a little startling that when my family went on vacation with several other families at the beach last year, I was caught off guard by grief. A young woman who was taking care of my house called to say that the goldfish had died. The previous fall, my youngest son and I had won Goldie the Fish by tossing a Ping-Pong ball into a shallow bowl at the Tennessee State Fair. For nine months I had tended to Goldie's needs as if it were a religious discipline. Because she was silent in her water world, I had to be mindful of her amidst all the noise in my house. So every night, just before I put my son to bed, the last thing we did was feed Goldie and make sure her tank was clean. It was a sweet time. I knew that snuggling my youngest boy at night and watching the fish grow was just a brief moment, like sand in my hand.

When I got off the phone and told my husband and friends about Goldie's death, they dismissed it with jokes. My son responded by saying, "Okay, can we go swim?" No one was even remotely trying to be mean; they simply couldn't imagine that it was any big deal. But as I was walking along the beach later that day, next to a million fish in the ocean, I realized I was grieving. Goldie's death meant that, in some way, the sweet time of having little children in the house who want fish was ending.

That fish taught me that we don't get to choose what we grieve. We can grieve getting pregnant; we can grieve not getting pregnant. We can grieve burying people we know and people we never met. We can grieve it all if we choose to open our hearts in that way. Goldie the fish reminds me that grief has many layers, and we don't have to apologize for what we grieve. Grief is the sweetness in our hearts released when we say good-bye to what we love and hold dear. We recognize grief in others, because it is so close to our own grief. Our grief connects us to all grief. It connects us to the world. It connects me to this stranger's family for whom I am coming to care.

Since grief is connected to all grief, sometimes we are grieving many things when one thing happens. There was a woman who called me to say she couldn't quit crying after her cat Gracie died. It was shocking to her, because she had always thought of herself as a strong woman. She had buried a husband and suffered many other losses but had never cried more. She said the cat loved her unconditionally, came to live with her when she was lonely, and often jumped in her lap just when she needed comfort. The loss of Gracie forced the woman to grieve the loss of everything. In mourning the cat she was mourning all her losses. I could imagine that through her tears, she had flashing recollections of many people she had loved.

I think that if one ages well, grief grows deeper and deeper. What we grieve in the present connects back to all our losses. This is a beautiful expression of how completely we are connected to God and all creation. My husband's Uncle Norm has a profound mind, a poet's heart, and an aging body. When the family gathers, he always reads a poem for the occasion. A short time after my husband's grandparents died, we all got together to celebrate a cousin's wedding. At the rehearsal, Uncle Norm stood up to read a poem he had written for the occasion and didn't get further than the title. Tears welled and he choked up. So did everyone else in the room. There was no need for words. Norm was experiencing the joy of the occasion while at the same time missing the matriarch and patriarch. He was connecting the dots of grief, bringing it fully and deeply into our hearts.

FOUR

twenty steps

The day of the funeral, I was not sure what to wear. The stranger had lived in Nashville but had come from the hills of Tennessee, so I thought it might show respect to dress more conservatively than I usually do. It is critical to show respect at funerals, especially if you are the minister.

Besides the cultural difference, there was another reason I was unsure of what to wear. Before I had gone to the visitation the previous day, I had eaten sushi in the car, and after the visitation I happened to glance in the rearview mirror. It was humiliating to realize I had some seaweed from the sushi between my front teeth. It also made me realize I was a stranger to them. If they were judging the book by its cover, mine showed a poor, sloppy priest. Maybe they thought I was not a very successful minister anyway, since I had all this time to spend with people I had never met before. It made me wonder if they wished they had gotten a man.

As I dressed for the funeral, I may have been trying to make it up to them by picking just the right outfit. I didn't want them to think I was bad priest because of a little seaweed in my teeth. My hope was to wear something that made me look like a minister, without scaring them because I looked like a minister. A collar was out. I chose chocolate cords, a plain white shirt, a cardigan I had found in the donated clothes pile at my church a couple of months before, and simple black heels. I put on sunglasses and carried notes in my prayer book about what I was going to say in praise of the woman I had never met.

The good thing about the seaweed was the fact that it had humbled me. If you're a priest, being humbled is a great way to enter a funeral. Being reminded that we are all dust is another step on that path of humility. That path has always been central to the walk of faith, especially regarding how we are to live and die as faithful pilgrims. Finding humility is essential for a meaningful life with God. Throughout his life, Jesus taught that there is blessedness in wretchedness—that in our suffering we are set on holy ground, and in our humbling experiences we find ourselves closer to God.

When Jesus went out into the world, he began by humbling himself and the people he encountered. In the inner circle of his followers at Levi's house, he humbled all the guests. The religious authority couldn't imagine why Jesus would be eating with his disciples and a bunch of sinners. Jesus didn't defend the character of his fellow dinner guests but simply said they needed him because they were sick. It must have been sobering for his followers to hear those words.

This walk in humility is central to our faith. Fifteen hundred years ago, St. Benedict of Nursia wrote what became known as the Benedictine Rule, describing how monks could live together in holiness. He called his brothers to ascend the ladder of humility by taking twelve steps, including reverence for God; doing God's will; being obedient to others; enduring affliction; and practicing confession, contentment, self-repproach, silence, and simple speech. In the seventeenth century, priest and theologian Jeremy Taylor wrote another rule about holy living. This time the walk in humility took an additional eight steps to total twenty steps, including having a right opinion about ourselves, being people of virtue, letting go of pride, practicing contentment, not making excuses for mistakes, giving thanks for our weaknesses, and submitting to God.

When you encounter humility, it is a holy experience. There was a woman who was part of the team I described earlier that went to Rwanda. She is a chemical engineer and manufacturing expert who left her job at a multinational chemical company and went into recovery. She came to Thistle Farms last year to serve the community and work on quality control and inventory. In everything she does, she teaches us about unconditional acceptance. When we were in the Rwandan countryside one night, traveling in a bus down a dark, two-lane highway, she suddenly said, "I hope that I find my purpose in life." I just laughed and said, "You'd better find it quick, because this may be it."

On that bus ride, she reminded me that our purpose is no more and no less than to love one another as ourselves. It doesn't matter if the person we are trying to love is dead or alive. It doesn't matter if the person is a family member or a stranger. Jesus speaks again and again about loving one another as ourselves. This teaching is so simple and yet so profound that letting it sink in is sometimes difficult. It humbles us. It takes losing things and people we love. It takes us tripping over our own feet. It takes the world reminding us sometimes. Sometimes it even takes having seaweed stuck in our teeth.

FIVE

angels and dirt

I learned in seminary that all of us grieve our own deaths when we go to a funeral. In my own ministry I've found that when I conduct a funeral, I can sense the people in the room considering their own mortality and the meaning of their lives. And I've learned that I can help.

Even though I had no prior relationship with the stranger's family, I could sympathize with the grief they were feeling. I could be an effective minister to the family and to a room full of people I had never met and I could speak with conviction about how God's love for us is our hope. I could connect with the congregation at this funeral, because it would be no different from the congregations gathered at the other fifty funerals at which I had presided. All the empathy I felt for the people, who like me wonder what it would be like to die, would help me bring a pastoral spirit to the funeral. All the empathy I felt for the family would make it possible for me to put together a meaningful liturgy.

Above all, I was beginning to understand how much I wanted the daughter to feel embraced by a compassionate community as she buried her mother. This special stranger had been a good mother, a fine friend, and a beautiful soul who had died too early. I was going to give my whole heart for the stranger at her funeral, because I know how hard and important it is to bury a parent well.

My own mother died after a long illness. She too had been a kind stranger to many people and an amazing mother and friend. It was about six weeks from the time they released her from the hospital into our care until the time she died. During those weeks I sat at home with her for several hours every day and kept a silent vigil every night. For anyone watching, I'm sure my siblings and I would have looked like faithful children, but to me, sitting by the bedside, it felt much more complicated.

My slow, private grieving had many layers. In the long silences by her bed, listening to her breathe, my mind would wander. I journeyed back to my childhood and replayed both the sweet times with my mom and some of the harder ones I thought I had forgotten.

I remembered my father's death in detail and the night my sister's boyfriend died. I remembered the time when my four siblings and I forgot to change the water in our three-foot aluminum-sided pool and all the water turned green. My mom got furious—I mean really furious—at our laziness and irresponsible ways, then stormed out the back door to take care of it herself. When she bent over to reach the drain, the side collapsed and she fell into the algae-filled pool. We were all pressed against the sliding glass doors, dying of laughter, until she turned back toward the house and we saw her face. Her hair was slimy, her brow was furrowed, and she was ready to pounce. As she marched toward the door, dripping, we all scattered, every child for herself. Years later, remembering that day, I sat beside the bed of my dying mother and laughed once again.

I remembered the times I had sneaked out of the house and the times I had lied to her, and I made my silent confession to her as my first priest. I remembered the times she had wandered away when I was little and left me to make my own way, which was sometimes full of traps and bad memories, and I gave her absolution as her last priest. I planned her funeral without meaning to and then hoped she couldn't read my mind.

There were times when I felt faithless and guilty. Some days I didn't want to be there at all, and some days it felt that it was just an escape from work and my two young sons. I could space out for long periods while I just sat there and watched, every now and then giving her a sip of something to drink. I would offer her a straw and consider the most basic tenets of faith I had held onto since childhood, wondering if anything had value in this world.

Once I passed a beautiful time by her bedside, imagining that I would leave my husband and children and job and go to work in Africa. I would fall in love with the work, with interesting strangers and the new land. I would trek up to Kilimanjaro, and life would be romantic again. I wanted the lives of my mom and me to be more beautiful and dramatic. We were just sitting there in her living room with a rented hospital bed and no background music. Her death was so slow. I found myself counting her breaths. I must have counted to a million in long, drawn-out seconds. I didn't want her to die, but I didn't want her to suffer, either.

I was so close to it at the time that I couldn't see how good and useful those weeks really were. I was able to grieve her life in detail, so that at her death I could celebrate it clearly. I think I remembered just about all the parts she let me experience. Sitting by her, I realized there were also parts that I wouldn't experience. We all die alone and no one knows us fully.

Several months after her death, I found a hair from her long brown braid on my couch. I cried all over again and knew that that grief, long after the death grief, was probably the most private and pure grief I had known. I imagined that my siblings were still grieving in private waves.

During the whole process of illness, dying, death, and remembrance, I was surprised by the prayers I said and the prayers I felt in my heart. First I prayed for her health and for the doctors and nurses. Once she was diagnosed, I prayed that she would die peacefully. In the weeks by her bed, I got to a place where the prayers were almost silenced. I felt such gratitude that she had been my mother, and I remember just saying, "Love you, Mom," like it was one of the sweetest prayers given to humanity. I wasn't asking for anything. I had no idea what to ask for.

My mom used to say that when she died, she would be dirt or an angel and both were useful. I had no patience with priests and friends coming to her deathbed with prayers for healing. It seemed wrong. It was clear she was dying, and I didn't want them to cheapen it by praying for a miracle and then saying that it wasn't God's will to heal her. There were over twenty priests coming by to pray, lay hands on her, talk to us, and just check in. All I wanted was for them to adore and love her and thank God for her life.

Just because someone is ordained doesn't mean he or she has a right to walk into the sacred space around a deathbed. Priest, rabbis, and shamans need to be invited into that space, either by virtue of their relationship to the people on the bed or near it, or because being there is part of their pastoral responsibilities. It can be awkward under any circumstances for the clergy to show up. It is exceptionally awkward if the family or the person dying doesn't want them there.

As a pastor, I have had some powerful visits with people, singing a hymn, offering a prayer, holding silences, giving communion, or anointing with oils. But I have had some pretty rough visits as well, when I was unsure about the situation and brought my anxiety into the space, tripping over myself while trying to do the right thing. The best we all do is to forget ourselves and to focus instead on the person who is dying, being present and open to those in need.

Once I went to what I thought was the deathbed of a beloved eighty-eight-year-old member of my congregation who was suffering from pneumonia. Because of my great love and admiration for her, I started to cry. She is an amazing woman, a perennial student who is wise in her questions and gracious in her listening. She says that she has finally come to understand what it means to live in a state of mindfulness. She says it keeps her filled with wonderment and the blessedness of not thinking about the past or a future yet to come. When I thought she was dying, instead of being concerned about her, I was sad for all of us who would lose her. I sat by her bed and prepared to serve her communion but only got as far as holding her hand and crying. Finally she patted my hand, told me it was all going to be all right, and said, "Why don't you just read Psalm 131?" When she recovered a few weeks later, I apologized. I told her that she was a good and gentle teacher to young priests like me, and I thanked her for showing me how to do a better job. "Next time I will even get through communion," I promised her.

A couple of years later she was knocking on death's door again, and I returned to visit her in the hospital. This time I brought some oils I had prepared, as well as communion. Before I could begin, she told me that she had never really understood what people meant when they described Jesus as a friend. "Now," she said, "it has made this part of the journey a little lonely." Immediately it made me cry. She was so clear and honest. I thought there might never have been a finer woman created. Again she had to pat my hand and ask me to read a psalm and to assure me it was going to be okay. She made it through that long winter too, and once again I have promised her that I will continue to learn and be more present to her the next time she is knocking on the door. We will share communion on one of the visits, I am sure. I also feel confident that if the tables are turned and she comes to visit me as I lie dying, she will be a strong presence for me.

When I die, I want someone to recite the prayers in the Book of Common Prayer. I want the person to

feel good about her faith and close to God. I want her
to say:

> Go forth, faithful servant;
> In the name of God who created you;
> In the name of the Son who showed you how to live;
> In the name of the Holy Spirit who comforts your soul.
>
> Amen.

SIX

sweet loneliness

During our initial visit at the funeral home, the daughter told me the story of her mother's death and how she had kissed her mom good-bye. She offered the story to me like a great legend. After she finished, I welled up. I may not have had a clue about who her mom was in life, but I admired how the mom had loved her daughter. I knew it would be an enormous task for the daughter to put her mother in the ground. She adored her mom, and it was going to be hard to let her go.

I wish we had to bury more strangers; it might make us feel differently toward the whole world. Often, there's not much of an emotional toll in hearing the story of a death from someone who never met the person who died. It is just a story. It can be an interesting story, but it doesn't affect you deeply, because it is not connected to your heart. The toll is a little bit greater when you hear statistics about people who died in war, famine, or natural disasters. It is horrifying and sad, but there is still distance and disconnection. But there is a huge emotional toll when you watch a person grieve the death of someone they loved. If that person is connected to the death story, all of a sudden the story sinks into your heart, whether or not you knew the person who died. Watching a person grieve someone they loved moves me toward compassion. It connects me to all the love I have ever lost in my life. It pushes against the edges of my heart and reminds me that there is blood in my cheeks and chest.

Not long ago I was called into a hospital's intensive care unit as doctors prepared to remove life support from a four-month-old baby girl from Mexico. The family needed a priest to say last rites before they would allow anything else to be done. When I stepped into the room, a wave of grief struck me. It filled the air, bathed faces in tears, and hushed everyone present. I knew immediately who the mother was, because a look of horror covered her grief. As I said a prayer and anointed the baby's face with oil, a translator repeated every phrase. Then life support was removed, and we waited for the baby's heart to stop. Waiting for a wave of grief is a powerful experience. Beyond time and space, it sets you at the burning bush, where all you feel is the presence of God.

I arranged for a great musician to sing at the funeral. The daughter had told me a little about the music her mother loved and suggested that we could play some recordings. I think that in worship, live music is better. If you have access to great singers, you ought to make use of them. This particular singer and I have been through much together over the past fifteen years. I am completely confident in his ability to bring a crowd together and his willingness to stand by me in times that are hard. I asked him if he could sing some old hymns and play his guitar. He had about twenty-four hours before he had to be back on the road, but he said he would be happy to give up his day off to drive out and sing for a woman he had never met. He had known grief in his own life, which made him willing to help another through hers. I told him I didn't know any of these folks but just wanted to do something nice for them, and he came.

In addition to the music, I decided to offer the first eleven verses of Psalm 139 and read the passage from the Gospel of Matthew about the lilies. Everyone in the world who loves scripture loves these two passages. They both speak of God's mystical love that permeates the whole universe, and they assure us we can rest in that wonderful knowledge.

LORD, *you have searched me out and known me;*
   you know my sitting down and my rising up;
   you discern my thoughts from afar.

You trace my journeys and my resting-places
   and are acquainted with all my ways.

Indeed, there is not a word on my lips,
   but you, O LORD, know it altogether.

You press upon me behind and before
   and lay your hand upon me.

Such knowledge is too wonderful for me;
   it is so high that I cannot attain to it.

Where can I go then from your Spirit?
   where can I flee from your presence?

If I climb up to heaven, you are there;
   if I make the grave my bed, you are there also.

If I take the wings of the morning
and dwell in the uttermost parts of the sea,

Even there your hand will lead me
and your right hand hold me fast.

If I say, "Surely the darkness will cover me,
and the light around me turn to night,"

Darkness is not dark to you;
the night is as bright as the day;
darkness and light to you are both alike.

The psalmist speaks in the first person about companionship with God on the journey back to God. There is an understanding, implicit in the writing, that first the psalmist must have felt alone to know why these words would be comforting to another. The psalmist knows that we walk the journey alone. There is not another human who can take this journey through death for us. It is one of the hardest things about dying: we are alone in it, except for the comfort people can offer us who are nearby and the faith that we can lean upon.

The psalmist names the fear of loneliness and comforts us that in the midst of it, God has not abandoned us. Coming to terms with our death in some ways means coming to terms with our loneliness. Loneliness comes into our lives in all kinds of ways. It takes root beside our other fears and makes us believe we are the only ones who feel it. Loneliness, I think, is universal and is an offering from God to keep us searching on the spiritual path. If we didn't feel lonely, we might feel settled and quit trying to wrestle with the questions that turn the stone to flesh in our hearts. I am amazed at all the kinds of loneliness in the world and how they affect our lives.

One kind of loneliness comes when we are literally alone; another comes from feeling alone in a crowd; another comes from searching our hearts to seek truth beyond all human society. All are humbling.

For years I have walked by myself in the woods and I love the feeling of being the only person on the planet. It's a peaceful path, and prayers come easily. I love walking, when the quiet is so pervasive that the gentlest of winds can be heard blowing in my ears like music. I rejoice at seeing spiderwebs that no one has broken. I celebrate the blueness of the morning sky and the knowledge that I may be the first to breathe it in without sharing it. Then, all of a sudden, I hear a strange noise from the undergrowth and my heart races. I remember I am alone and feel vulnerable and worried. My sister says the fear is the same whether the tiger is in the bushes or not. I believe her. It always takes me a minute or two to calm my heart and return to a more thankful and peaceful state of mind. After those experiences I walk more humbly, with lots of gratitude, and a little faster.

The kind of loneliness that comes from feeling alone in a crowd takes place in our hearts. It can happen at parties, or at church, or in malls, or at games, or anywhere people are gathered. It comes from wanting to feel that we are unique and that our voice matters. In this world filled with billions of people, sometimes we feel that it would not make a bit of difference whether we were here or not. It's a sick, lonely feeling. In Cairo, Egypt, it was surprising to see that even though most of the women were dressed in black with head covers, there were hundreds of shoe stores. I'm not talking about a couple of stores; there were some streets on which it appeared that every other store was a shoe store. At first it seemed incongruous. Then I realized, shoes were the only thing that set the women apart. If you're draped in black, shoes can speak volumes. Through them, a woman could probably let people know her style, taste, political preference, age, health, and a hundred other things about herself. The shoes kept the women from loneliness. They became a source of individuality, bonding the women through conversations about "Where did you get those shoes?"

To me, the loneliness of truth seekers seems like the noblest kind of loneliness. It comes from the hearts of people who can take the long view. They see themselves on the surface of the earth, in orbit with other planets, looking out into infinite space. This kind of loneliness reminds you that there is no up or down in an infinite space where a sphere flies through the galaxy. In this space, truth has no dimensions and time wraps in on itself. Here all thoughts are free to explore the depths of heaven and earth, and no one gets to make the rules. It leaves you feeling small, and wondering what the point of making out another grocery list could possibly be.

SEVEN

getting dressed

Driving to the stranger's funeral, I imagined people getting ready for the service, sorting through their feelings as they sorted through their outfits. Some were coming out of a sense of obligation. Others might be trying to remember the last time they saw her. Some might have come because they had worked with her or had known her for a long time. But some would be coming because they loved her. I imagined the daughter getting dressed and wondered if she thought much about what she was wearing. Maybe she went out and bought something new. Maybe it was something she and her mother had gotten together. There were a hundred different people in their homes and offices preparing for the service. The service would not be in the news or stop the flow of business as usual, but for these few, it was going to be an occasion.

The florists would be delivering the last flowers, and the people at the funeral home would be vacuuming the maroon carpet. All the preparations are part of the liturgy. They are part of the sacred act and maybe more worshipful because there is not an audience to observe. Once I sat down an hour early for the funeral of a distant friend. The volunteer altar guild set up flowers, prepared communion, and trimmed the wicks, oblivious to my watchful eye. Three or four altar guild members had tasks to take care of before the service began. As the women entered the chapel, each separately stopped in front of the coffin and, like a sweet mother showing her love, adjusted the white pall covering it.

Grief is complicated; it isn't as clear-cut as the five stages they teach you about in seminary and not as easy as selecting the right outfit for the funeral. You don't necessarily feel shock, anger, sadness, loneliness, and then acceptance. People feel delayed grief, subconscious grief, and a million other nuances of grief. There are some folks who don't understand why they are grieving, because their relationship with that person has been broken for a long time. They can't figure out why they are feeling a new loss. Maybe they are grieving the loss of what they never had and the chance of ever having it. The death is simply another reminder of that loss, which they know like the back of their hand. It is still grief.

I sat once with a friend who buried his mother, a woman who had been pretty horrible. In some parts of my friend's mind he was sad his mother had died alone, but there was another part of him that knew his mother had carved her own destiny. If you are mean, the chances of dying alone probably increase exponentially. If you are poor and mean, the chances are probably even greater. When your mother is abusive and hurtful, grief feels strange. People come up and say, "I am so sorry about your mother," and you feel conflicted as a part of you wants to scream, "I have felt sorry about my mother for years."

There are the slow deaths that people have been grieving for months or years before the passing, such as the faithful servants who have cared for a parent who had Alzheimer's for ten years, or for a daughter with spina bifida, or for a spouse with several bouts of cancer. I think their grief is complicated, because even though they are now grieving the loss of the body, they had been grieving a million losses along the way. Some may grieve losing the job of caring for their sick loved one and trying to establish a whole new life. Others may grieve all the time lost in caring for the person.

Then there are the people who are grieving such horrible and tragic deaths that the lives they had known before the death have categorically changed forever. These people live on and have a new life, but the one they have known is done. Their grief sets them on such holy ground that it is hard to walk near. It is an enormous privilege to be allowed to walk on part of that ground with them. I have witnessed what people at funerals go through, and for some it is close to labor at a birth. They will have to learn everything all over again. They will learn to eat, sleep, go to the grocery, attend a church service, get through a holiday.

When I think about people getting ready for this funeral, I imagine a collage of rich and complicated thoughts bringing different textures and meanings to the death.

When my mother died, my sister Pam was about to deliver her fourth child. Pam sat by our mother's deathbed with the rest of us, counting my mother's final breaths as she felt Emma's feet stirring against her belly. During the funeral she experienced her first labor pains. Two days later, in the hospital, she was still in labor. The nurse told Pam to let the baby come and not to hold onto her because of grief for her mother. It is humbling to know that grief can be so powerful it can stop a baby from being born.

When people are grieving, they look graceful to me. No matter what stage they are going through or how complicated the grief is, the spirit appears to be close by. People who experience the death of someone they love seem to walk for a long time with a different gait. On any given day they are feeling a million different things and are led by where they are in relation to the person who died. Some of their toughest times happen months after the death, when all the flowers from the service are gone, the cards have trickled to a halt, and the world is ready for them to jump back in. That is when grief will catch them like a wave and pull them down. Eventually they learn to trust that soon they will be back on top of the water, breathing again. When people are grieving, all the pettiness and mundaneness of the world evaporate around them. They need space to think and move without judgment. Even though they may look lost or afraid, they are being led by their heart and can trust where it is taking them.

It is the people who are not able to grieve who seem lost to me, the people who are using all their energy trying not to be sad or not to be angry or not to deal with the consequence of death. Sometimes when I have been with such people, I can see a pulse under an eye, or a smile that comes at strange times. Sometimes it surfaces in a dismissive tone or in isolation from people who once were close. It really is heartbreaking. These people have a right not to grieve, especially in the presence of others, but it seems exhausting.

None of these thoughts about grief are intended as blanket statements about all people. I am simply thinking about the people I have known in and through death for the past seventeen years of my ministry. Certainly there are some commonalities, but there are also particulars, such as estates, unfinished business, and the deep things that people hold private in their hearts. Grief is always unique and always a surprise. It is a surprise when people break down for no reason. It still is a little startling when people get irritated at nothing while planning a service. It is really surprising when humor peeks its head around the corner and gives everyone a break from the relentless onslaught of grief.

I have truly loved some of the times that are funny. I love the fact that humor is a part of death and dying. I cherish the times I have sat by the bed of people who were dying and they have had the courage to make a joke. I remember one time in particular.

It was about a month after a funeral that I had helped conduct. The family, a beautiful and awe-inspiring group, had invited people who had been with them through the death to come to their house for dinner. We had been so close over the previous month, sitting up at night, telling stories, sharing a drink, and combing hair. We were combing hair because somehow that season, God only knows why, lice nits had taken root on many heads of hair in Nashville. In the midst of all the grief, the lice had found places to land, so we just kept combing hair and comforting one another.

When I got to the house, there was a white package wrapped in a beautiful gold ribbon sitting on the dinner table. During supper they invited me to open the package. My eyes welled up, because I knew it would probably be a framed picture of the person who had died. "I'll open it later," I said with teary eyes. "Open it now," they insisted. I gently unwrapped the package, and inside I found a metal lice comb they had found at Walgreen's. We all burst out laughing. It was a moment of grace. It wasn't that the death didn't still sting, or that the grip of death had lessened; it just meant we were going to make it to the next day.

EIGHT

scars

The funeral home was on the outskirts of Nashville. It took about thirty minutes to drive there, through old, familiar streets. Memories like early-morning fog sat close by and kept me company.

During the drive I thought about how many strangers there are to me in my own town. I can travel through this tiny part of the world and feel at home, connected to buildings and signs. But if I reflect on people, I am aware that almost all the people who live here are strangers. If I can't love these strangers as my brothers and sisters, I will live like a stranger in my own land.

Driving through the area reminded me of a nearby store where once, when I was a little girl, I couldn't find my mother. I was scared because I didn't know a soul around me, and so I decided to hide. I climbed into some trash cans that were stacked for sale nearby and crouched low until sometime later I heard my mother's voice calling to me, and I stood up. She asked me why I was ducking inside a trash can and pointed out that it made it much more difficult to help me. At the time I couldn't explain it to her, but it felt safer to hide in a trash can than to be alone in the presence of strangers. I was afraid, and all I could do was trust that she would find me, no matter what.

Hiding is something all of us do when we get scared. Instead of standing out in the open and asking for help, we cover ourselves in shame and fear and wait for someone to come searching for us. Looking back, I bet there were nice folks in the store who would have helped me find my mother, but I was under some kind of red terror alert.

Feeling alone among strangers is scary. The more recent phenomenon of violence by terrorists plays on that fear, and one of its ripple effects is that we become afraid of all strangers. Instead of realizing they can help us, we live in fear that they may approach or harm us. We teach our children to fear strangers, and yet the truth is that kids are usually hurt by someone they know. The person who will beat them, abuse them, and undermine their innocence is usually a friend or family member. When you work with women who were abused as children, you learn that part of their struggle is to recognize that those they trusted were the very people who hurt them.

In my own life, it was a family friend. Anything but a stranger, he was a leader in the church and a friend to my mother after my father died. No one hesitated to leave me alone with him. He took full advantage of his friendship and made me feel estranged from others because of what he did.

I remember the times when he sexually abused me, and those memories have affected every aspect of my life and how I understand the world. I know that without those memories, I would not have the same ability to talk about forgiveness as I understand it or have the same compassion for women on the streets. After years of therapy, writing, speaking, and forgiving, mostly I still think of it all as living in the most private part of my heart. Sometimes it is so secret, I wonder if it is real. It feels too tender to show the people I love, and too important to show the people I don't know.

There are so many people walking around this planet like me. They share a common story, but they lived through the events in the story alone. During the most frightening events with the man who abused me, I was completely by myself, and I couldn't believe that someone else could ever understand my experience. The man could cause me terror just by walking into the room, even if the room was filled with people. That private experience of terror hung on for years, robbing me of innocence and joy.

Those events are a sacred truth for me. They make me want to guard my heart to protect that truth. But it doesn't have to be that way. Our secrets don't have to make us strangers. I believe we can hold our truths in the light and honor them in one another without trying to fix them or change them.

In my life it has been strangers who have led me out of deserts and side paths. I have been rescued from the ditch several times by compassionate strangers I have met along life's roads. That is why when two women from the Sudan walked into my office last fall, I was glad for the opportunity to be a good Samaritan to others, and I tried to greet them as friends. I could tell they needed a stranger to offer a little help.

They had been on a long and arduous journey from a bloody war that had created an entire generation of refugees. They told about the death of most of their family, the destruction of their village, the separation from their siblings and friends, their flight to Egypt and the brutality they faced, the process of becoming refugees, and their arrival in the United States. Now, years later, when the women were living safely in Nashville with their own children, they were feeling called to return to their village and build a school for the orphans of war. They said that God had been merciful to them, and this was an expression of their gratitude. Having been given mercy from the war, they needed to make meaning out of all the suffering. The scars on their legs were reminders that none of us can walk fast enough to get away from the pain.

While they were describing their arduous journey, the old prayer welled up in me: "God have mercy on me, a sinner." I prayed that God would forgive my arrogance and indifference to all the suffering strangers called refugees and that God would allow me to hear the cry of others. We made arrangements for their journey home, making sure they had gifts to offer their neighbors when they returned.

As I drove to the funeral, I thought about an old friend who was one of the wisest men to walk this earth, who has

cared for strangers in his own way. He loves this planet—
every tree, animal, and person. He was an outdoor educator
in Maryland when I met him. He was always on a crusade
to recycle and live more simply. I lived in the basement of
his house in 1986 while I was working as an intern for Bread
for the World, an organization in Washington, D.C.
Wherever he drove, he was in the habit of stopping and
picking up strangers. His wife and grown children would ask
him to please stop helping strangers, because one day they
might kill him. He just said, "I'd rather be dead than live in
a world where I can't help a stranger." He lived out that
simple and profound truth. About five years later, he was hit
by a car while picking up trash on the side of the road. He
has had to learn to walk again and uses a brace, but he has
never wavered in his love of the stranger. No one could
dent his firm belief that the only way to live was to love the
stranger.

last respects

I took my time sitting in the parking lot at the funeral home. I was making some notes about the order of the service and making a concerted effort to observe the other strangers going into the funeral home. I wanted to watch the folks in groups of two or three come together to form a congregation. This would be the only time this particular group would ever gather, and I didn't want to miss anyone.

So I sat there in my minivan and observed them. I watched all the life that was unfolding before me, and I watched the mourners, all strangers, file in.

"They were coming to pay their last respects," as the saying goes. I am not sure what that means, except that respect for the dead is sacred. We dress up the person in the coffin. We drape our own bodies in black, the respected color of mourning. We hold silences and give up our seats to those who were closer to the deceased. It is the last way we can show them that they have been honored and that they are not alone in their grieving. There is nothing else to do. We can't make it better, so we just show one another respect and try to bring dignity as a parting gift.

The funeral home looked incongruous to me. It sat next to a putt-putt and go-cart park. The building seemed out of place. Funeral homes should be back a ways from the street, set apart so people have space to grieve, like the space around an airport so planes have plenty of room to take off and land. I have seen car lots with big sale signs and balloons next door to cemeteries, and I've thought the balloons must feel intrusive to families during a burial. But there are makeshift memorials and cemeteries all over the world that pop up in the midst of life. One of my friends says that her father's grave now overlooks the Beaman bottling company, instead of the old tree that offered shade to the mourners when they buried him forty years ago. I have seen small cemeteries fenced in next to interstates, on the back lots of farms, and in the middle of cities. There are crosses on the side of the road marking places where loved ones died. There are sweet statues set in gardens and parks, and benches that bear the names of old visitors. These memorials all seem to preach the same message: Everything keeps going, but we have to honor people and the land we bury them on.

All the new strangers I saw filing into the funeral home were a part of the other stranger's life, and I wondered what sweet secrets they had shared. Did the stranger live differently with different people, care for some more than others without their knowing it? Who among the people walking through the doors knew her dreams and fears? Was she a stranger to some of these friends? I loved looking at the people and wondering how all the connections were made. It was like looking at a tapestry that had taken her a lifetime to create.

Watching them, I felt lucky because life wasn't passing me by. I wasn't going to wake up one day and wish I had paid attention. I would never have to think back and wonder if I had ever lived as if I were dying, because that was exactly what I was doing at that moment. All that mattered, sitting in my minivan in the parking lot, was that I could love people and I could be loved.

TEN

the tomb

Before the funeral, the singer and I sat in a conference room next to the visitation room where the family and friends were gathering. The conference room was the place where families would meet the funeral director and make decisions about how they wanted the person buried.

The place, like the meetings the place held, felt awkward and contrived. On a table was a stack of pamphlets and brochures, along with a Bible and a calculator to figure out what the family could afford. One of my favorite brochures advertised a motorcycle escort service for the loved one's final ride, including a group of riders who would come wearing tuxedo-like shirts, black pants, and "a single spur." I wasn't sure why one needs spurs for a motorcycle, but somehow the idea of a single spur seemed like a noble kind of tribute. It had that single-rose-in-the-empty-seat feel. At the bottom of the brochure was the service's tagline: "Wherever we go, we hear the words echoed over and over. 'Now that's how I want to go out.'"

Tackiness and funeral homes go together like theater and glitter. It's hard to put on a show for the deceased without seeming saccharine, contrived, or at least compromised. Even so, I don't understand why so many funeral homes have sacrificed taste and beauty for uniformity and convenience. Most cemeteries don't even have tombstones; they have flat markers for even mowing. There are no trees and shrubbery allowed around graves, just a single bundle of plastic flowers attached to the marker. These cemeteries look ridiculous compared with the old graveyards attached to churches and synagogues, which have a wonderful variety of stones covered with moss. Some graveyards have wooden markers obscured by time. All of them make more sense, emotionally and theologically, than "it's easier to mow this way."

The worst example I've seen is an indoor mausoleum attached to a funeral home I visited last year. The mausoleum was four stories high, and on the ground floor I noticed a sign that said "Christ's Tomb," with an arrow. Of course I had to follow it, and it led to a plastic garden with a pond full of koi fish. At the far end was a door cut out of formed concrete. When I opened it, I found a wrought-iron fence, with a crown of thorns casually resting on one of the fence posts. God have mercy on us.

After the singer and I went over the details of the service, we were left with an awkward silence, similar to the feeling of waiting for a doctor or for an important call. In that moment, my grief turned a familiar corner and faced its close cousin, fear. Sometimes death really does scare me when I think about how cold and final the whole thing is. I hate the idea of being buried or cremated. It is so final.

Several years ago in Ireland I read the epitaph on Yeats's tombstone. It seemed as though he had captured the wave of feelings washing over me. He said, "Cast a cold eye / On life, on death. / Horseman, pass by." When we stop and think about death, fear is usually lurking close by. When I sat by Yeats's tombstone getting my picture taken with my kids, I thought about how he had composed those lines when he was alive. His clarity and boldness had the effect of pulling people in, even as he was telling them to go away.

It was a beautiful day in Ireland, and people were picnicking nearby. The rolling hills and the newlyweds strolling along spoke of the sweetness and the joy of life, and yet in the midst of it, death felt close.

In Guayaquil, Ecuador, there is a huge cemetery with high-rise mausoleums that look like condos. It covers a hillside and holds hundreds of bodies in eight-story concrete temples with plastic flowers adorning them. If you walk down just one aisle of the cemetery, you can see thousands of bodies stacked in close proximity. Standing there, you can feel the reality of being surrounded by strangers in death, and you can't help feeling vulnerable and lonely. When our group from Nashville drives by that tall, wide cemetery on our annual visit to run a clinic in a village about 150 miles north, I think how much I don't want to die. I don't want my body stacked like a brick in a wall with thousands of others on an overcrowded hillside. Our group is on a trek to stave off death and keep folks healthy. The huge graveyard preaches loud and clear of death's power and its reality in all our lives.

It is even more humbling to drive by one of the biggest cemeteries in the entire world. It is in Cairo, and in addition to dead people, the cemetery has become home to almost a million others. They are called "the living dead." A long time ago, families would come to the cemetery and visit their beloved for days, so they made resting places with shelters to cover them. Now, homeless and desperate strangers have taken over burial plots just to have a place to rest their heads. They are literally making their homes over the dead bodies of strangers.

One of my fears about dying is that I may be forgotten. What if no one remembers me after I pass? The thought makes my whole life feel like a passing shadow. Last summer my family spent a week in Key West, Florida. One day we took a tour of Ernest Hemingway's home. Key West has claimed the famous writer as its own and has preserved everything from the books he once read to random pictures of him as a younger man with friends. His home feels sacred. The possessions seem valuable because they were attached to him. They're sealed behind glass and roped off, so his memory remains alive for the sake of history. I want to believe that the memory of each of us, like the belongings of Hemingway and other famous people, is valuable to God as a part of creation. One of the beautiful things about sacred texts is that they remind us we are not forgotten: we will be remembered by God.

Death might be less foreboding to me if I had a clearer vision of heaven. When I think of what heaven is like, I am silenced. I have never been able to make sense of God's love for all humanity by using a formula for salvation from any single faith tradition. Instead, I just keep studying and reflecting how various ideas and traditions are a part of God's mystery, unfolding through words, revelation, and tradition. Applying these truths in the face of death, all of us are called to surrender our lives to God, follow the path, and proclaim without fear the truth that we can trust our whole lives to God. We are to trust that God will carry us to the eternal side of time, despite our fears of death and dying.

I believe there is a heaven and it is for all people. Beyond that, I think it is all just musings. There is a part of the Gospels, though, that to me provides a glimpse of what heaven must be. Jesus said that God loves the sparrows, the most common of birds, and knows when they fall. God loves humanity so intimately that God even knows the hairs on our heads. We do not have to be afraid when we die because God knows us. We are more valuable than sparrows and will never be forgotten by God.

Heaven is God's memory. We are preserved in the memory of Love that is big enough to contain all creation for all time. No one is forgotten, because everyone is beloved. Nothing can touch the truth of God's love for us or erase us from the memory of God.

Our own memories are slender threads in the span of time. Not only are we dust, but even our memories are dust in this world. I can imagine the words in Hemingway's books vanishing off the pages in a few hundred years. I can imagine the tombstone of Yeats and the great mausoleums crumbling to dust. Our memories are not our own; they are as fragile as the neurons that carry them. My mother's memory turned to a sponge twelve years ago as she was dying. At her death, she couldn't remember the name of a soul on this earth. That a person we love doesn't even get to remember that we love them seems particularly cruel and humbling.

I heard a priest remark once that nothing is sadder than someone who has lost his memory. But losing our memory doesn't mean we have been forgotten. Even the Jane and John Does, whom no one can name when they die and who lie buried in the paupers' cemetery that we call Potter's Field, are not lost to God. They live in God's memory. I have seen my mother's spirit in hawks and dreams and have felt her living presence for years. She is part of God. While we will never know the mind of God, we can know what it is like to be remembered by God. That knowledge gives us peace and courage in this world and hope in heaven. It is wider and deeper than any memory we have ever held. And with that knowledge, I can move from fear and dread to a place of anticipation and hope.

I have always believed that if we remain faithful, no matter the fear, grace will come. As we pass the cemetery in Cairo and round the next curve, we catch sight of a golden dome. As we move beyond the cemetery in Ecuador, we see the shadow of a crow's wings on a Teca tree leaf. I don't have to cast a cold eye, as Yeats suggests. Love, not death, has the last word.

ELEVEN

a single hawk

In the funeral conference room there were also pamphlets describing casket choices. My family has always been firmly in the camp, "Why bury money?" Get the plainest and cheapest casket or urn you can buy. It is better for the environment, saves your family money, and says something about where you put your treasure. It also makes it easier when the funeral director offers casket options. "Just the cheapest, please," you say, and then the conversation is over.

We buried our mother in an urn that cost about seventy dollars. It was a source of pride for all five of her children. We knew she would be proud that we didn't cave in and buy her something really expensive to stick in the ground. My father was buried in a plain pine box, which my mother loved to talk about. She would tell us that since he was a priest, we could have picked any casket for free, but she had picked the cheapest. "That is what your father would have wanted," she told us.

I know, in fact, that it isn't what my father would have wanted. He would have wanted to be alive and watch his children grow and walk us down aisles and whisper how hard it was to see us so beautiful and independent. When I contemplate my mortality and realize that everything around me is temporal, I don't care at all what kind of urn is chosen for me. I just want to think that I loved well while I was alive.

I admire the cemetery at St. Mary's, a retreat center near Nashville, because of its simplicity and beauty. Each grave is marked by a cross with the name and year of death. If you are paying close attention, you'll notice that the markers are in chronological order, not according to rank or family. People are buried according to the order in which they die. This seems holy and right. Around the simple cemetery, tall pines stand like sentries, keeping a vigil for women who loved the world. It gives me hope that in simplicity we can find our way to God.

About a month ago I attended the funeral of a friend's friend at the Cathedral of the Incarnation in Nashville. I had never met the young man who had died. When I sat and remembered all the funerals for friends I had attended, I cried anyway, along with a thousand other people who had been chatting and visiting just moments earlier. We cried because the violin played a solo, because the bulletin was made of the same cream-colored paper used at all Cathedral funerals, because the prayers were old, because the family was crying, because the afternoon light shone through the stained-glass windows, and because we were human. We cried because in remembering that our brother was now dust, we were remembering how close to dust all of us were. It is good and right to cry at funerals, even for people we never knew. Maybe it is the last gift of the dead to the living, to let us sit and cry for how tender life is sometimes.

When I die, I want to be buried in Potter's Field near the Jane Does of Nashville and near a woman I buried a few years ago. Her daughter had lived at Magdalene, the organization I helped start. When her mother died the daughter asked me to officiate at the funeral. The mother had survived poverty, being ostracized by her family for marrying an African American, and being left by her husband, and she had stood by her daughter during some horrible times. Her funeral almost undid me.

The daughter could afford only the bare minimum for her mother's funeral. After the service, we weren't allowed to follow the hearse because they said it would cause traffic problems, and we hadn't hired an escort. So we got lost on the way to the city cemetery and were calling each other on cell phones, trying to find out how to get there. The city cemetery lies between the sewage treatment center and the gas storage facility. It is surrounded by chain link fencing and a few small maples. It is the place where they bury all the Jane Does who don't find their way home in this world. When we got there, the funeral attendants were already taking the mother out of the hearse. I asked them to stop so we could pray before they put her in the ground. It felt as though we were intruding on their job, that we were the strangers. They did what we asked, though, and we stood and cried and said the Lord's Prayer just like at any other funeral. In fact, if we really believe that our souls have life beyond the ashes of our bodies, it doesn't matter where we are buried. But that cemetery still haunts me.

Once while hiking near a cemetery for veterans, I saw a funeral I will never forget. I happened by as a hearse arrived, and the grave diggers, those blessed strangers, were stubbing out their cigarette butts. It would have been comforting to see a flag flying at half mast, but the flag was blowing in the wind at its highest point. It would have been pleasing to observe a grieving woman dressed in black, but all I could see from the trail were two grave diggers finishing their smoke and chatting as the hearse arrived with the newly dead, feet first. This veteran was surely asleep for eternity now, unaware that there were no mourners or family, but somehow I felt that I had become the congregation.

They buried him without eulogy or a rite beside soldiers he had never met, and the sky was diamond blue. They didn't have a gun salute. There were no velvet seats to ease the pain of the grieving. There was just a body being lowered. I know that he didn't feel the sting, but I wanted to get up and ask the grave diggers to stand with me for a minute out of respect for his service and his solitary life, but I was silenced by the passing shadow of a single hawk. God once again had gently but firmly set me in my place. The single soaring hawk across an infinite clear sky was a perfect tribute. The veteran wasn't being laid to rest as a stranger but was in good hands. I needed to remember the starkness of death, and I needed to remember we are never alone in death.

T W E L V E

the thistle

During the planning of the funeral, it gave me pause to think that this woman was just one stranger in a world of billions. It was like trying to love just one star in a clear night sky. All we can do is keep loving the ones in our view.

All the world's great religions have teachings about strangers. The lessons point to the underlying blessings we receive in offering hospitality and compassion to the stranger. There are rules in the Judeo tradition, for example, about our obligation to the strangers among us and a reminder that we come from wandering Arameans. We are required by our faith to let the widows and orphans glean the fields. We are strangers in a strange land, the psalmist calls out.

Throughout the Gospels, the poor stranger has a special significance. Whatever we do to the least of the strangers and friends among us, we are doing to God, so if we love the stranger, we are loving God. We are asked to be like the foreigner in the story of the good Samaritan, merciful and loving and going the extra mile. As Jesus and his followers roamed the countryside healing strangers, they were showing that the act of helping those we don't know is like a sacred act of worship. We may be strangers to each other, but we are not strangers to God; so we can be assured that if we try to love each other, God will be pleased. Because of what I've learned in the Gospels, I know that the act of offering a funeral for a stranger gives me a way to love and be loved by God.

Over the past eleven years, I have worked with women coming off the streets, through the Magdalene organization. As I have traveled in Nashville and around the world doing that work, I have learned two things. First, I am completely indebted to strangers, those who have given us the means and the grace to keep going, as well as those who have come to live in our community homes and have trusted the community to be their sanctuary. Strangers have given us the means to keep going, providing furniture for homes and gas for cars. Strangers have shown up with exactly what we needed when we didn't even know how to ask. Strangers have left the streets they have known for a decade, never looking back. Second, I have become a thistle farmer.

If I could pick an epitaph for my grave, it would be this: "Consider the thistle." Labeled by most people as a weed, the thistle grows in the streets and alleys where the women of Magdalene have walked. It has a deep taproot that can shoot through thick concrete and survive drought. In spite of its prickly appearance, the soft purple center makes the thistle a mysterious and gorgeous flower. For these reasons and more, when we started a nonprofit business seven years ago, to be operated by and for the women of Magdalene, we called it Thistle Farms. Now as I travel, I look for thistles wherever I go. Slowly but surely they have become a sign to me of grace and abundance. They grow all over the world. And now I realize I have become a thistle farmer.

The travel and the work leave me feeling knee-buckling grateful. It is the kind of gratitude that comes from brokenness and the mercy people have offered me along the way. It comes from knowing death, tasting fear, and seeing God's compassion in all things. Thistles are there for any-one, but they feel like a present, free and wild. To be a thistle farmer is a way of walking in the world, a way of loving the world, a way of understanding one's own worth in the world. As a thistle farmer, I see the world as a plentiful field with no borders, owners, or strangers. Anyone can harvest the thistle's beauty in alleys, in abandoned lots, along railroad tracks, and in the poorer sections of town. Searching for it, we learn that beauty can be found in all of creation and that nothing is left to be condemned.

When Magdalene was created, we saw it as a testimony to the truth that in the end love is the most powerful force for change; it is stronger than what drives women to the streets. Those streets are hell, I'm told, and I've never met a woman there who hasn't been raped or left destitute. For me, that suffering creates a moral imperative for our lives of faith. The moral imperative is not confined to people who share our doctrinal beliefs, nor is it bound by national borders. It applies to people of all races and ages. It affects all our communities, the culture we live in, the health of the world, and the way we raise our children.

The issue is the suffering of others. It should cause all of us to stop and try to soothe their pain. We should do this even if we feel overwhelmed, scared, or judgmental. There is an amazing story in the Gospels describing how Jesus stopped to mix mud and spit to heal a blind man. The message seems to be that it doesn't matter if we have all the resources, if the problems seem far greater than our resources, or even if we don't know the person suffering. In the face of pain, we stop and use what we can to be a part of the healing.

The women of Magdalene, on average, have more than a hundred arrests each and were first sexually abused between the ages of seven and eleven. These women don't end up on the streets by themselves. It takes a community of people, both strangers and friends, to put them there; it takes drugs; it takes a culture that continues to think we can buy and sell others at no cost to their well-being or our own. It takes a belief in legalizing prostitution, a step that would do no more than benefit men. It takes the women's numbness and dismisses it by labeling it as a choice.

Strangers have become friends through the bath-and-body products we manufacture at Thistle Farms. These products have become our link across the United States and with programs globally. Everywhere we travel, we meet brothers and sisters who are healing from the same scars found on the women in Nashville. Meeting those people, we recognize the scars on ourselves. Dorothy Day, a beloved saint, says that you cannot help a sister or brother in need without getting naked first. All humanity knows suffering. When we remember that, we realize that mercy runs deeper than abuse, and we learn the freedom of forgiveness, the miracle of recovery, and the power of loving without judgment each day.

Last year in Rwanda, we began classes on how to make candles and soap. While waiting for the wax to melt, we huddled on couches and shared stories. Periodically we would run over to check the pots. It felt as if the melting wax somehow held the promise of freedom. As the wax was transformed into a liquid, we would pour it over wicks and add sweet fragrance and color. The candles would then be sold for more than the women had once offered themselves for. In making the candles, we were packaging a dream of new life, and so we kept checking the wax, stirring the pots, and offering a prayer. We gave thanks that it might be possible for the women in the circle never again to sell their flesh to a stranger. As the wax set in the molds, we prayed that our hopes would melt into our own hearts.

Those candles seemed like mud mixed with spit in the eyes of a blind man. They were all we had, and we prayed that they would help. The women in Rwanda are no longer strangers to me, but friends, and their cottage industry, though vastly different from ours, is thriving.

golden hoops

I waited until about fifteen minutes before the service and then walked into the visitation room. I said a prayer with just the daughter, her friend, and a couple of relatives. Then the family left to be seated, and the funeral home staff came in. They asked me if they should remove the woman's jewelry before they closed the coffin, and I told them I didn't know much about the family's wishes. They left the room to go look up their instructions again. And just like that, I was left in the visitation room with dim parlor lamps, floral arrangements, and the body of this stranger.

It was just her and me. I was going to be the last person in the whole world who saw her elegant body with the simple gold hoop earrings and the fitted pants suit, and still I was a stranger. I stood by the casket and whispered a prayer for her. I imagined that her last thoughts had probably been of her daughter, so I said a prayer for the daughter on her behalf. I wanted my final words to have meaning. All I could think of was "I promise I will not forget."

By this time I knew I was learning a powerful lesson about life, not my life or her life, but life itself. It was a lesson about trust and letting go, but the thoughts were random and fast. There were pictures of her all over the room, and I had glimpses of how in so many ways she was like everyone else, except for the subtle differences that mark us like fingerprints. She was immaculate in every picture and had eyes that could smile. She seemed confident and friendly toward the camera. She seemed to be strong, similar to a steel magnolia, but more refined and resilient. I was beginning to know her, and she was becoming less and less a stranger in the walk we were taking together.

I stood there and imagined the pain the daughter must be feeling. It was the pain of loving another human being. We are called to love God with our whole heart and to love our neighbors like that as well. This is a tall order. It takes a lot to love someone with your whole heart. Sometimes I think about loving my husband with my whole heart. I try, but it's hard not to hold a piece of yourself back, to save yourself from the grief of kissing someone you love good-bye. The truth, of course, is that the pain of *not* loving with your whole heart hurts more; still, it's hard to love someone completely and know that they will die someday or they will have to bury you.

I had visited a friend the week before whose cancer had recurred. He had lost all his hair, was being fed through a tube, and had dropped so much weight that his skin looked heavy. He was a talented, young, compassionate, and beautiful person. Looking at him, I felt anger. His suffering seemed painful and unbelievably cruel. He wept when he talked about how he wanted to be like a prince for his bride. It was hard to watch, and it made me wonder if I was going to be strong enough to hold that much pain.

Sometimes I am not okay with death. Sometimes I am scared of what I will lose in this world and frightened about the pain of dying. There is no way to sit with someone who is so sick and not be overwhelmed by the grief you can feel coming. It's like watching a huge wave, knowing you'll have to dive straight into it or it will pound you face-first into the sand.

I know that death is a part of life, and until we accept it, we are not free to live. When we love people, we cannot avoid it. We can choose the pain of loving people, even in death, or we can choose the pain of living without love. I will always take the first kind of pain, but sometimes it is bigger than I am. God bless all the lovers, the mothers and daughters, and the friends who are carrying the pain of saying good-bye.

FOURTEEN

lilies on the grave

The funeral director came in and closed the lid of the coffin. Then we entered the chapel. I was walking ahead of the coffin, like a drum major in a parade, like an actor in a movie. My role was to be unwavering in my faith and confident in my leadership. I was leading the coffin under the banner of heaven. I was wearing my white alb with a solid white stole, carrying the Book of Common Prayer and my notes.

As we processed up the center aisle, I realized I had forgotten my Bible and started glancing around for one to use. I got a panicked feeling, and suddenly all connection to the people and the moment was lost. Fearing I wouldn't be able to find a Bible, I tried to remember the gist of the passage in Matthew about lilies and decided to just quote pieces of it instead of reading the whole thing. I had a cold, sweaty

feeling in my palms. I continued to walk slowly and pur-
posefully without looking around.

When I reached the podium, I glanced over at the
singer. He could tell I was feeling lost and a little panicked.
There was dead silence in the room in the split seconds
spent looking around for some kind of Bible to use. Then,
thank God, I saw a white leather King James Version inside
the podium. Taking a few seconds to gather myself, I fumbled
through the pages to Matthew. When I found the passage, I
wiped my hands on my alb and decided to paraphrase it,
since the King James Version is an old translation that,
while beautiful, is different from the one I use.

Then the music started. The singer's voice rose up, fill-
ing the space with spirit and a richness that only melodies
can bring. I offered silent prayers of thanksgiving for his
unwavering gift. Words sometimes limit our range of emo-
tion, but music lets our feelings soar. It expands our hearts
and lets us feel deeply. After the song, I offered prayers asking for comfort for the grieving family, for the promise of
resurrection, and for the hope that love brings.

In the silence between prayers, my mind drifted. I
thought about eternity. I noticed the pain on the faces of

the family. I wondered if I had left my sunglasses on my head. I pondered how heaven seems surreal. I saw that the daughter was weeping. I wanted time to stop and then prayed it would jump ahead. Part of me just wanted to walk away, reminding everyone that the stranger's spirit had already broken free from her body and there was no reason to go through with the service.

I know an older priest who died and had requested there be no funeral. He had been ordained for fifty years. God knows how many funerals he had conducted, and in the end he wanted to skip the ritual for himself. I can only imagine why. Maybe he was critical of what other priests said in funerals and didn't like the idea of people speaking for him. Maybe he knew all the hypocrisy and conflicting thoughts we carry into funerals, and it made him skeptical. Maybe he felt that we try to turn mortals into saints with a simple amen. Maybe he was just tired.

I read Psalm 139 from my beloved Book of Common Prayer, then opened the King James Version of the Bible and tried my best to remember the lilies of the field as I preferred them. As I finished the reading and closed the book, I looked out into the room full of strangers and wondered what I would preach. I had to trust the words that had come to me to celebrate her life, with the few lines I had jotted from her daughter the day before. Of course, it's impossible to sum up a life in words. All I wanted to do was paint a few brushstrokes that would add to the picture of her. I wanted to say something about how her life reflected the gospel. I wanted the daughter to feel that her mother's spirit had been celebrated.

So I preached my sermon for this sweet stranger. I talked about how I was grateful to be included in the family circle. I told them how perfect it seemed to read about the lilies of the field. Somehow, in all the troubles of the world, our Lord took time to consider the lilies. They represent the lavish way he loves us and everyone in the world. Lilies are a name we give to beautiful babies. Lilies are what we use to decorate our finest altars. Lilies surround us in death. They're a gift. They're perfect. And they need nothing else. To add anything is called gilding the lily. It is unnecessary. This woman we bury today is a beautiful lily of God. There's something about a lily, about her, about her life, that symbolizes what is beautiful about God. In the lily and in her, the beauty is in the details.

How grateful she must have been to travel the world and marvel in God's abundant creation. In the picture of her on the program, she is looking out at the world with binoculars around her neck. The binoculars show how much she must have loved the details lavished on our creation. She wanted to see them all. In the photos of her life, she looks lovely and tender. But she never equated tenderness with weakness. In addition to beauty and tenderness, there was humor in her spirit. That too was a sign of God's mercy and benevolence.

Lilies bloom and die and somehow are sweeter and more precious because they are temporal. She bloomed like a lily and graced each one of you with her presence. She was a beloved friend and a devoted wife and a gifted worker and a sacred mother. People say she died with no unfinished business and with praise for a life well lived.

There is another gift offered to us as we gather in her honor. We have come together to know her more fully and to see her more clearly. Now we can share our individual love and see how beautiful it looks in the field of love she sowed during her life. She has offered us the gift to grieve her lavishly. For love's sake, you have a right to grieve what is beautiful and consider it and see how it points you to the love of God.

After the sermon we sang another song, and I walked over to the casket and offered a prayer:

You only are immortal, the creator and maker of humanity; and we are mortal, formed of the earth, and to earth shall we return. For so did you ordain when you created me, saying, "You are dust, and to dust you shall return." All of us go down to the dust; yet even at the grave we make our song: Alleluia, alleluia, alleluia.

Give rest, O Christ, to your servant with your saints, where sorrow and pain are no more, neither sighing, but life everlasting.

The prayer was for the repose of her soul and peace in heaven. It thanked God for the gift of life. It asked for God's triune blessing upon the body and upon the souls of all the departed. Finally, it asked for comfort in the hope of resurrection.

We ended the service with a beautiful song. When I turned away from the casket and faced the family, I swear the light in the chapel had changed. It was less harsh. Everyone looked softer. Just a degree of change in the sun's height, the time it takes to offer one prayer, can change the lighting in a room dramatically. I took a deep breath and asked the congregation to stand. Six of her closest male friends carried her casket out the front door of the funeral home and into the hearse. As we walked into the broad daylight, the reality of death stung my eyes along with the bright sun. Its meaning hit me, and I could feel my legs get a little shaky.

getting lost

We placed the stranger's body in the hearse and got into our cars, then lined up and waited for the funeral escorts who would lead us to the cemetery. There we would lay the body to rest and begin the real work of mourning.

It took a few minutes to line up, and we were fidgety about getting started. We waited for the sedans with the two small purple flags on the hood and the yellow flashing light on top to take us where we needed to go. The funeral director was standing beside my car, which was parked behind the daughter's car, which was parked behind the hearse.

"Do you want some water?" asked the funeral director.

"Sure," I said, and then asked what the delay was about.

Instead of answering my question, she told me why she was working at the small funeral home and assured me that the funeral was beautiful and that we did a wonderful job. She had worked for a larger funeral home that had been sold, and so she had lost her position. Now she was working at the small place until something better came along. I could see that for her, it was just a job.

"What is going on?" I asked her again.

"I think the escorts got lost," she said. "But I don't want to upset the daughter."

I felt my heart sink. No matter how hard you want it to go well, something gets screwed up. If it's not forgetting the right translation for the beautiful text about the lilies, it's the escorts getting lost. I tried to imagine how escorts get lost in the first place.

Climbing out of the car with my robes still on, I went over to the daughter and asked if she needed some water. I gave her the bottle that the funeral director had just given me, then I told her it seemed that the escorts were lost and asked what she wanted to do. After discussing options, she said with poise and resolve, "Let's just go." So we did.

It was about a thirty-minute drive, complicated by the fact that we had no escorts to direct traffic or help us through the intersections and winding roads. Somehow it seemed fitting. We travel the path of grief alone. We figure out how to negotiate death without much guidance, even from professionals.

Along the way another beautifully symbolic thing happened. There had been a drought for a long time, and yet for ten minutes the rain fell. I took the rain as a sign of God's presence and blessing. I felt that we were led, even without an escort.

It was overwhelming to see how many strangers stopped and offered their respect as the procession drove by. Thank God we cannot avoid strangers in death. They are the bearers of grace. When they paused for the procession, all traffic on the two-lane road had to stop. It felt like pure thoughtfulness for the needs of others. As they turned their eyes toward us, I was filled with gratitude. The strangers were everywhere, surrounding us with assurances that we wouldn't get lost.

I remembered the funeral of John Frazier, who was buried when I was eighteen. He was a volunteer fireman in Nolensville, Tennessee, and when his procession passed, all the volunteers from the fire department lined the streets with their helmets in their hands. It was so powerful to see the men grieving with respect and dignity. They didn't need to say a word. Their silent presence spoke volumes.

One of the most remarkable funeral processions I ever saw was in a small city in northern Ecuador. The procession was on foot, so all traffic had to stop completely. A hearse led the procession, followed by a group carrying the casket on their shoulders and a couple of hundred mourners. Instead of holding the casket, the hearse was lined with huge speakers that blasted grief in surround-sound, drowning out all other noise. It felt like the tropical air itself was mourning. The procession took an hour out of our day and blessed our whole journey.

I presided over one funeral that included a procession down a four-lane road. During the procession, several cars tried to pass in the left lane. When they did, some of the cars in the procession eased out to block them, offering a last defense for the dead.

By the time we arrived at the cemetery, we had been driving almost forty-five minutes. During that time, I had gone over the funeral several times in my mind and thought about what I might change if I had to do it over again. I knew, though, that it probably didn't matter. The daughter was more likely to remember the texture of the carpet than a word I said. She would remember the songs, but not that I changed "thou" to "you." She might remember the musty smell of the room or the old tiled ceiling, but she had probably already forgotten that the escorts didn't show up. As we drove, I'd been able to see the back of the daughter's head in the car ahead of me. I didn't envy her what was coming next.

We pulled up to the plot. The grave was a gaping hole with a mound of dirt nearby. There was a canopy, with several chairs draped in blue velvet. The workers had set out green plastic turf in several areas to hide the machinery and the reality of brown earth.

I remembered a time in the spring of 1997 when I visited my father's grave. I noticed that the tombstone had become covered with moss in the thirty years since his death. Kneeling in front of the tombstone, I took out my earring, the only tool I could find. I bent the end of the earring and used it to clean the moss from the lettering of my father's name. Six months later, I buried my mother beside him.

It is so hard to lay a body in the ground. A wave of sadness came over me as we waited for the rest of the group to park and gather around the plot. The pallbearers lined up at the back of the hearse, then walked the casket to the metal slats resting over the hole. The pallbearers looked so dignified and strong standing there in their black suits. I didn't know the name of a single one, but I could sense their strength and faithfulness.

We watched in silence. We gathered at the graveside. Standing there, I knew that whatever came and whatever had already transpired was okay. Everything is a sign and a blessing. At the grave, mourners only see God. The rest fades into background.

SIXTEEN

being found

In the end we are all buried by strangers—not just metaphorically, but specifically and realistically. Most of us do not know a person who digs graves for a living, so the chances of a stranger burying us are close to one hundred percent.

Grave diggers handle the casket and take care of the hard manual labor. I have never seen them as being emotionally engaged or worried about the people grieving nearby. They seem matter-of-fact, and they treat all caskets the same. After all, bodies are pretty much the same after death. Grave diggers would need to have some gallows humor about their work and what it means. But when all is said and done, they are the ones who preside over our deaths.

As the grave diggers stood close by and watched, we sang "Amazing Grace" with full sunlight on our shoulders.

Then we said a prayer as they began their task. First they adjusted the casket's position so it would be lowered into the center of the hole. Then they wrapped a chain around the concrete shell holding the coffin, secured it with a hook, and, using a crane, began to lower the coffin. Twice during the process, the coffin hit the sides of the hole. The grave diggers realigned everything, cranked it up a little, and started it down again. There was a clicking noise as each link in the chain passed through the crank. Once the body and coffin and concrete casing were in place, they rolled up the plastic turf and began moving the equipment. Finally they stepped away so we could put the first handfuls of dirt onto the grave, with a final prayer:

In sure and certain hope . . . through our Lord Jesus Christ, we commend to God our sister, and we commit her body to the ground; earth to earth, ashes to ashes, dust to dust. The Lord bless her and keep her, the Lord make his face to shine upon her and be gracious to her, the Lord lift up his countenance upon her and give her peace. Amen.

When I dropped dirt into the deep square hole containing her body, I cried. The tears came from a place where deep calls to deep, from a wellspring that lives in all of us and fills us with wonder. I love the water of tears. Those are the waters that set the captives free in Egypt, that we are baptized in, that connect us to the holy and living God.

The grave diggers dumped the rest of the dirt from the flatbed truck into the hole. As they spread and smoothed the dirt, people hugged and then scattered. I stayed like a sentry near the grave, keeping watch, trying to make sure everything was done right. I stayed while the grave diggers laid the flowers from the funeral over the new plot, while they loaded their shovels and slats onto the flatbed, while the funeral home employees took the blue velvet off the folding chairs and walked away in a small group, talking among themselves. I stayed until no one would notice when I took off my vestments and folded them around my prayer book.

I looked around for the daughter. She was off to one side in the center of a small circle, receiving comforting hugs and words. She didn't need me to interrupt her. I never saw her again.

Everything that is alive dies. It's a hard truth to grasp on a sunny day. It takes a whole life and lots of patience to understand and let it rest in peace.

SEVENTEEN

the blessing

I left the cemetery alone. Wrapping my vestments around the prayer book, I laid them on the passenger seat and drove away in silence—not a silence because I was alone but a deep and full silence from all that I had just experienced. I had loved someone I never met, and I knew I wouldn't see the family again. It was the beginning and the end of our friendship.

I had an hour to spare before picking up my children from school, and so I drove slowly. There was no background music to ease the silence. The cars passing me were filled with strangers. They were people I didn't have a clue about, going on with their day as all of us do when strangers die. It is the only way life can go on. We can't stop for all the births and deaths, or we would never move. Instead, we stop for some of them and then try to hold a space for people to mark their own grief. I don't know how the planet stays in orbit with all the heavy spirits in the world. There must be another hundred funerals taking place around the world right now, and I am not even counting the animals.

As I drove back toward town, my mind drifted to my husband; he must be what I am most afraid to lose. As I thought about him, crossing my fingers that he lives longer than I do, I passed a Target store and pulled in. Now, Target may seem like a strange choice as a place to process grief, but it works for me. It's big, with lots of distractions, and I can stock up on stuff for my house, which gives me a sense of caring for my family. That day, I went toward the jewelry section. I remembered my husband saying his watch had broken, and I wanted to pick up a new one for him.

I bought a fifty-dollar Timex watch for him and needed to pick up some other items before I checked out. After the woman in the jewelry section got the watch out and I decided to buy it, I asked if I needed to buy the watch before getting my other items.

"Usually yes," she said, gazing at me with kind eyes behind thick glasses, "but I trust you."

"But I'm a stranger," I said.

She said, "Well, you have to trust strangers sometimes."

I wanted to hug her for preaching what I had been feeling. Instead, I thanked her and assured her I wouldn't let her down.

When we die, we become dirt or angels, and both are useful. It seemed to me that it all comes down to a matter of trust. I have to trust God and, when I meet death, jump as gracefully as I possibly can across the shore of time. All will be well. It doesn't really matter if I am buried by strangers and laid down to rest with strangers. I am surrendering my life and my death to God. I will hope in resurrection.

On my most recent journey to Ecuador, our group hiked in the Andes to what felt like the top of the world to see a waterfall. We were silenced and humbled by the magnitude and power of the water, which tossed huge volcanic boulders like skipping stones. I wept at its majesty and thought of all the time I had wasted wondering if the stone was rolled away at Easter. Standing at the base of the waterfall, I could see how easily stones can be moved.

I have seen water move rocks. I have seen thistles break through boulders. If water and flowers can move stones, surely love can. In death there is a deluge of love. It cleans everything out to make room for a soul that has been set free. In that deluge, the stones of our hearts and tombs are rolled away, time and eternity meet, and we are laid to rest. I imagine that if there is some state of consciousness in heaven, I will not seek my husband, my mother, or even my sons. I will be looking for God.

Nothing can compare with a belief in resurrection. It is what sets us free to love the stranger and move with grace through the world. I believed in resurrection completely as I walked through a cemetery near that waterfall in Ecuador. It was on a green hillside, with rough stone tombs on which hand-lettered epitaphs had been painted. Some of the names were gone, and some stones were beginning to erode.

As I studied the tombs, a small lamb walked out from behind one of them. Life continues after death. The sun rises. The flowers bloom in spring. Love never dies. I accept resurrection, just as I accept death.

Now I lay me down to sleep
I pray the Lord my soul to keep
If I should die before I wake
I pray the Lord my soul to take.
God bless Marcus, Levi, Caney, and Moses.
God bless the strangers who offered mercy to me.
God bless the strangers I walked past.
Amen.

Interview

An interview with Becca Stevens, founder of Magdalene, a residential community for women with criminal histories of drug abuse and prostitution

How did Magdalene begin?

In 1997 we opened up a community called Magdalene. The idea was that it would be a small community for a few women who have had a really rough time—who have had criminal histories of drug abuse and prostitution. These are women who have trouble working through institutional systems, school systems, family systems. Systems have not been kind to them. And the idea was literally to lavish them with love and give them a safe place to live for a couple of years where they could really heal. There would be no authority figure, no live-in staff, no rigid way to be. We invited five women to come in—women who all had at least a ten-year history on the street and a hundred arrests on their records—so it wasn't like they had a lot of other choices or places to go. And we raised the money so they could live together and work on their recovery and work on their spiritual life and be together. It was the most beautiful experiment I've ever been a part of. The women came; and they stayed clean and sober, and all of us were changed in the process.

Why do you think the Magdalene model worked?

Community had a lot to do with it. These women had not ended up on the streets by themselves; it had taken a whole community to get them there. So it was going to take a community to bring them in. We didn't take any government or state money. This was really about the community giving in gratitude to the women, offering everything for free. The women came and lived in the program, and everything was given to them. The idea was that whatever you get from us, just give it back to somebody else. And that's been the model, and it's worked that way for years.

Tell us about Thistle Farms.

Each year Magdalene opened up another house, until we had four residences. And what we realized was that women were getting clean and sober and were having powerful experiences in community. But economically they were still very, very vulnerable, and they would go back to old relationships that were dangerous, or they would take jobs that put them in harm's way. We wanted to give them a safe work environment, where they could get something on their resume and learn how to work and still have that sense of community. So we started Thistle Farms, a cottage industry run by and for the women of Magdalene. It was no accident that we decided to make bath and body care products. The idea is that the products heal your body, and you're offering these products to others to heal their bodies. We believe that in the eyes of God it doesn't matter who's the giver or receiver, but that love is present in the exchange. It's like a quilting circle. You know, you can imagine women sitting around and telling their stories and sharing their joys and sorrows, but instead of making a quilt, we're making bath and body care products.

What have you learned from Magdalene?

All of us need community. All of us need sanctuary—safe places to go to be ourselves, to be heard and not judged.

And in being heard, somehow there's healing. It's not just that you're healing me. It's that in telling you the story, I find God's healing. We've witnessed it for a decade now, being a part of this work. And that is the truth of my life. What I'm the most grateful for in my ministry is my communal experiences in Magdalene. I'm more faithful than when I started out. I'm more hopeful about women and about recovery and about community and about how generous a community can be. We have never, ever gone without. As I said, we are completely dependent on the generosity of others, and it's always been there. And that's a beautiful, beautiful testimony to how powerful community can be.

Learn more about the work of Magdalene and Thistle Farms at www.thistlefarms.org.